WILD ANIMALS

HONEY BADGERS

BY ABBY DOTY

WWW.APEXEDITIONS.COM

Copyright © 2026 by Apex Editions, Mendota Heights, MN 55120. All rights reserved. No part of this book may be reproduced or utilized in any form or by any means without written permission from the publisher.

Apex is distributed by North Star Editions:
sales@northstareditions.com | 888-417-0195

Produced for Apex by Red Line Editorial.

Photographs ©: Shutterstock Images, cover, 1, 4–5, 6, 7, 8–9, 10–11, 13, 14, 15, 20–21, 22–23, 24–25, 26, 27, 29; iStockphoto, 16–17, 18–19; Media Drum World/Alamy, 12

Library of Congress Control Number: 2024952634

ISBN
979-8-89250-548-2 (hardcover)
979-8-89250-584-0 (paperback)
979-8-89250-652-6 (ebook pdf)
979-8-89250-620-5 (hosted ebook)

Printed in the United States of America
Mankato, MN
082025

NOTE TO PARENTS AND EDUCATORS

Apex books are designed to build literacy skills in striving readers. Exciting, high-interest content attracts and holds readers' attention. The text is carefully leveled to allow students to achieve success quickly. Additional features, such as bolded glossary words for difficult terms, help build comprehension.

TABLE OF CONTENTS

CHAPTER 1
SNAKE HUNTER 4

CHAPTER 2
IN THE WILD 10

CHAPTER 3
BRAVE BADGERS 16

CHAPTER 4
LIFE CYCLE 22

COMPREHENSION QUESTIONS • 28
GLOSSARY • 30
TO LEARN MORE • 31
ABOUT THE AUTHOR • 31
INDEX • 32

CHAPTER 1

SNAKE HUNTER

A honey badger searches for food. Soon, it spots a large cobra. The snake hisses. The badger charges.

A honey badger can sprint up to 19 miles per hour (30 km/h).

Honey badgers often hunt Cape cobras.

The honey badger swings its paw. Its claws cut the snake. The cobra lunges at the badger. But the snake's fangs don't break through the badger's skin.

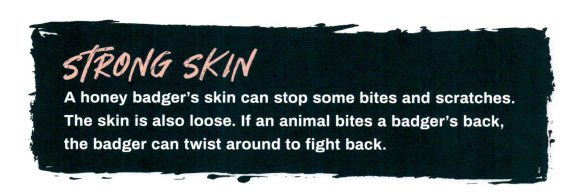

STRONG SKIN

A honey badger's skin can stop some bites and scratches. The skin is also loose. If an animal bites a badger's back, the badger can twist around to fight back.

A honey badger's thick skin can block bee stings and porcupine quills.

The snake strikes again. This time, **venom** flows into the honey badger. But the badger keeps fighting. It bites off the cobra's head. The badger has its meal.

FAST FACT

Cobra venom is usually deadly to small animals. But honey badgers often survive it.

Honey badgers eat many kinds of animals. Snakes make up about 25 percent of their diet.

CHAPTER 2

IN THE WILD

Honey badgers are **mammals**. Much of a badger's fur is black. A large gray-white stripe goes down the animal's back.

Adult honey badgers are about 3 feet (0.9 m) long. Most weigh between 14 and 30 pounds (6 and 14 kg).

A honey badger's sharp claws and teeth can crack a tortoise shell.

A honey badger's legs are short but strong. The front feet have long claws. Honey badgers also have sharp teeth.

FAST FACT
Honey badgers often dig deep **burrows**. Some burrows go 5 feet (1.5 m) underground.

Honey badgers sometimes sleep in holes found in trees or rocks.

Female honey badgers travel about 6 miles (10 km) each day. Males travel up to 17 miles (27 km).

Honey badgers live in parts of Africa and Asia. They are **adaptable** animals. So, they can live in different habitats. These include dry deserts and wet rainforests.

STINK BOMBS

Honey badgers can release smelly liquids. The animals use the smells to mark their large **territories**. Honey badgers may also drop stink bombs when in danger.

Honey badgers often survive attacks from larger animals.

15

CHAPTER 3

BRAVE BADGERS

Honey badgers will eat almost anything. They usually hunt live animals. Sometimes, badgers steal **prey** from other animals. Or they eat dead animals.

Honey badgers sometimes eat plants and fruit.

Honey badgers travel long distances to find food. A strong sense of smell helps with the search. The animals may find food underground or high in the trees.

FAST FACT

Honey badgers often eat **larvae** from beehives. That's how the animals got their name.

Honey badgers eat all parts of an animal, including hair, bones, and feathers.

Honey badgers have few **predators**. Lions, leopards, and hyenas may attack them. But honey badgers are hard to kill.

FARMERS VS. BADGERS

Humans are the biggest danger for honey badgers. The badgers sometimes find food on farms. So, many farmers and beekeepers kill badgers to keep them away.

Honey badgers may rush at predators to scare them away.

CHAPTER 4

LIFE CYCLE

Most of the time, honey badgers live alone. But the animals come together to find **mates**.

22

To find mates, male honey badgers follow the smell of females' pee.

A mother honey badger usually has one cub at a time. The cub is born hairless. After a few weeks, it grows fur.

A mother moves burrows every few days. She carries her cub in her mouth.

FAST FACT
Newborn cubs weigh just 7 ounces (0.2 kg).

Honey badgers live up to seven years in the wild.

A honey badger cub stays in a burrow for three months. By six months old, the cub is fully grown. But the mother still cares for it. The cub stays until it is more than one year old.

LEAVING THE BURROW

After three months, the mother teaches her cub to hunt and dig. She also lets the cub eat animals with weak venom. Over time, the cub is able to withstand stronger and stronger venom.

An adult honey badger can dig a 10-foot (3-m) tunnel in just 10 minutes.

COMPREHENSION QUESTIONS

Write your answers on a separate piece of paper.

1. Write a few sentences explaining the main ideas of Chapter 3.

2. What feature of honey badgers do you find most interesting? Why?

3. Which animals are honey badgers most likely to eat?

    A. lions
    B. bee larvae
    C. hyenas

4. How long does a honey badger cub stay with its mother after it is fully grown?

    A. seven weeks
    B. less than six months
    C. at least six months

5. What does **lunges** mean in this book?

*The cobra **lunges** at the badger. But the snake's fangs don't break through the badger's skin.*

   A. moves away from
   B. moves toward
   C. stays still

6. What does **habitats** mean in this book?

*They are adaptable animals. So, they can live in different **habitats**. These include dry deserts and wet rainforests.*

   A. places where animals live
   B. plants that animals eat
   C. places that animals avoid

Answer key on page 32.

GLOSSARY

adaptable
Good at changing to fit new situations.

burrows
Tunnels or holes that animals use as homes.

larvae
Insects that have hatched from eggs but have not yet changed to adults.

mammals
Animals that have hair and produce milk for their young.

mates
Pairs of animals that come together to have babies.

predators
Animals that hunt and eat other animals.

prey
Animals that are hunted and eaten by other animals.

territories
Areas that animals or groups of animals live in and defend.

venom
A poison made by an animal and used to bite or sting prey.

BOOKS

Downs, Kieran. *Wolverine vs. Honey Badger.* Bellwether Media, 2021.

Koster, Gloria. *Coyotes and Badgers Team Up!* Capstone Press, 2023.

Marie, Renata. *Honey Badgers*. Kaleidoscope, 2022.

ONLINE RESOURCES

Visit **www.apexeditions.com** to find links and resources related to this title.

ABOUT THE AUTHOR

Abby Doty is a writer, editor, and booklover from Minnesota.

INDEX

A
Africa, 14
Asia, 14

B
burrows, 13, 26

C
claws, 6, 12
cobra, 4, 6, 8
cubs, 24–27

D
digging, 13, 27

F
fur, 10, 24

H
habitats, 14

M
mammals, 10
mates, 22

P
predators, 20

S
skin, 6–7
stink bombs, 15

T
teeth, 12

V
venom, 8, 27

ANSWER KEY:
1. Answers will vary; 2. Answers will vary; 3. B; 4. C; 5. B; 6. A